In Touch

Telephone and Fax

Angela Royston

Heinemann Library
Chicago, Illinois

Designed by Visual Image
Illustrations by Visual Image
Originated by Ambassador Litho Ltd.
Printed in Hong Kong/China

06 05 04 03 02
10 9 8 7 6 5 4 3 2 1

Library of Congress Cataloging-in-Publication Data
Royston, Angela.
  Telephone and fax / Angela Royston.
     p. cm. – (In touch)
Includes bibliographical references and index.
Summary: Presents an overview of the use and function of telephones and
fax machines.
  ISBN 1-58810-067-7
  1. Telephone–Juvenile literature. 2. Facsimile
transmission–Juvenile literature. (1. Telephone. 2. Facsimile
transmission.) I. Title. II. Series.
  TK6165 .R68 2001
  384.6–dc21
                                    2001004636

Acknowledgments
The Publishers would like to thank the following for permission to reproduce photographs:
pp. 4, 5 Stone; pp. 7, 13, 25 Telegraph Colour Library; p. 8 Philip McCollum; p. 9 Ed Pritchard/
The Stock Market; pp. 10, 28 Corbis; p. 11 Photodisc; p. 12 Sheena Verdun-Taylor; p. 14 Chris
Honeywell; p. 15 Science Photo Library; pp. 16, 24 R. D. Battersby; pp. 17, 22, 23 The Stock
Market; p. 18 Greg Pease/The Stock Market; p. 19 Peter Poulides/The Stock Market; p. 20
BT/Marcomms Image Library; p. 21 BT Corporate Picture Library; pp. 26, 27 Nokia; p. 29 Ericsson.

Cover photograph reproduced with permission of Trevor Clifford.

Every effort has been made to contact copyright holders of any material reproduced in this
book. Any omissions will be rectified in subsequent printings if notice is given to the Publisher.

Some words are shown in bold, **like this.** You can
find out what they mean by looking in the glossary.

Contents

Communications

Communications are different ways of talking to people. Television, radio, telephone, fax, newspapers, and the **Internet** are all forms of communication.

Telephones

This book tells you how the **telephone system** can connect your phone to any other phone in the world. You can talk to friends and family, even if they are far away.

It is fun to talk on the phone! You can call anyone who has a telephone.

This woman is using a fax machine. It copies and sends what is on the page, but it does not send the sheet of paper.

Telephones at work

At work, people often use telephones to discuss their work, arrange meetings, or find out information.

Phone lines can also be used to send information as a **fax.** This is a way of sending words and pictures by phone.

Telephone Systems

Most telephones are connected to other telephones by telephone wires. But there are too many telephones for every one to have a wire linked to each of the others.

Local exchange

Instead, each telephone is linked to a local telephone **exchange.** The local exchange can take a call and send it on to any other telephone in the same area.

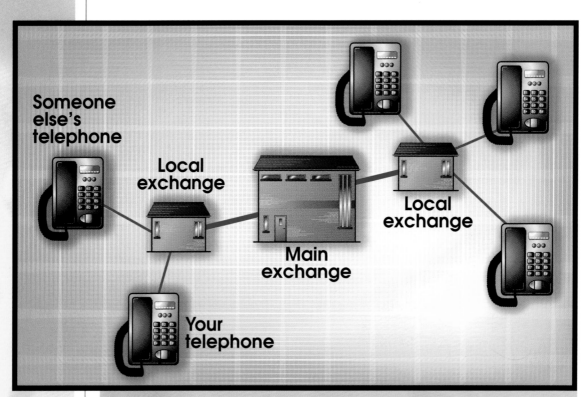

Each call goes through a local exchange on its way to the person you are calling.

Main exchange

A main exchange links several local exchanges, forming a **network.** Every telephone in the network can be connected to any other.

All the main exchanges are linked together to form a huge network that covers the whole country.

Operators working at a telephone exchange help people to make calls.

International exchange

International exchanges pass calls from one country to another. They let you contact people on the other side of the world. You can call just about anyone, anywhere, at any time.

At the Exchange

Many people work for telephone companies. **Operators** help with calls, and **accountants** send out bills and collect payments. Telephone engineers repair telephones and lines.

Computers

There are too many calls for operators to handle them all. So the **telephone system** uses computers in many different ways.

Bad weather can damage telephone lines and poles. Engineers check and repair the damage.

Computers can show if there are any problems in the telephone system that need to be repaired.

For example, computers control most telephone **exchanges.** The computers can work day and night. When a call comes in to the exchange, the computer sends it on to the next exchange, or to a local telephone.

Paying for calls

Whenever you make a call, a computer at the exchange times the call and figures out how much it costs. It stores the information and sends a bill, usually every month. You pay only for the calls you make, not for the calls you receive.

Sending Messages

Telephone calls can travel in several different ways. Most calls are sent as electrical **signals.** They travel along telephone wires that are bundled together into thick cables. In some places, the cables are hung from tall poles. In other places, they are buried under the ground.

Some cables are dropped to the bottom of the ocean! These stong cables can carry calls from one country to another.

This ship lays telephone wires along the bottom of the sea. Thick steel cables protect the wires.

Radio waves

Telephone calls can also be sent as **radio waves.** These waves are sent through the air by a radio **transmitter.** They can travel long distances before they are received by an **antenna** or dish.

Satellites

A **satellite** is a kind of spacecraft. Its many antennae pick up radio waves from one transmitter on Earth and bounce them back to another. Messages can be passed along through several satellites, all the way around the world.

Communications satellites send and receive signals for telephones, television, and radio.

Making a Call

To make a call, you have to dial the number of the person you are calling. Every telephone has a number that is different from all other telephone numbers.

Telephone codes

Every telephone number is made up of different codes. The computers in the telephone **exchanges** recognize the codes that you dial and send your call to the correct telephone.

Your telephone has keys for the numbers 0 to 9. You use the keys to dial the number you want.

Ringing and answering

The person you have dialed needs to know that you are calling! His or her phone rings. You can hear it ringing at the other end of the line.

Busy signals

If someone is already using the phone you have called, you will hear a busy signal. You will have to try to call again later.

A company's switchboard is a private exchange. An **operator** connects you to the right person.

Hearing Sounds

When you talk on the phone, the sound of your voice is changed into electrical **signals.** When the signals reach the other phone, they are changed back into the sound of your voice.

How sounds become signals

When you talk into the telephone, your voice makes a tiny piece of metal **vibrate.** A tiny microphone inside the telephone changes the movement of the piece of metal into electrical signals.

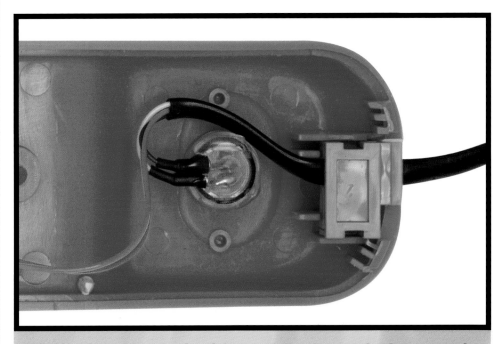

The microphone inside a telephone helps send your voice to the person you are calling.

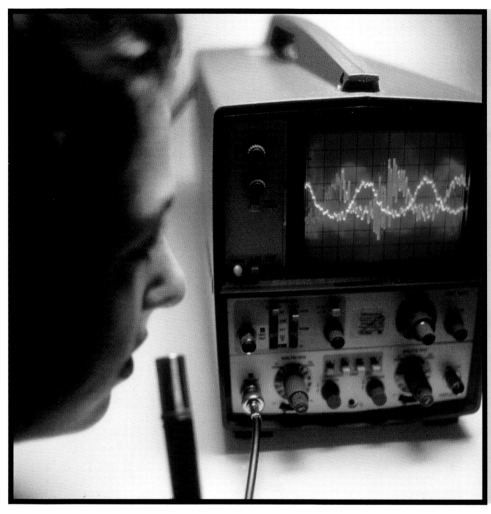

This microphone changes a voice into signals that show on the screen.

Signals become sounds

The signals travel through the telephone **network** to the phone of the person you are calling. A tiny loudspeaker in that phone receives the signals and vibrates another piece of metal. The loudspeaker makes a sound just like your voice!

This may sound complicated, but phone signals really travel very fast. It is almost like talking to someone in the same room.

Telephones Today

At one time, telephones could only send and receive telephone calls. They all had to be connected by telephone wires.

Today, phones can send and receive many kinds of messages, and many are not linked to a telephone wire.

Mobile phones

Mobile phones do not use telephone wires. They use **radio waves** to send and receive messages. Some messages are sent by voice. Others are typed in as words and letters.

The **antenna** at the top of a mobile phone can send and receive messages carried by radio waves.

Answering machines

If you cannot answer the telephone when it rings, an answering machine connected to the phone can record a message from the person calling you.

Other links

Telephones can also be connected to other machines, such as computers and **fax** machines. They can even be hooked up to televisions!

A computer linked to the telephone can be used to find out information from the **Internet**.

Millions of Calls

Most calls travel along telephone lines, but ordinary telephone wires cannot handle very many calls at one time. Luckily, there is a faster way to send them.

Special bundles of electrical wires called **fiber-optic cables** can connect main telephone **exchanges.** Fiber-optic cables carry telephone messages in the form of light beams.

This fiber-optic cable carries messages as very fast flashes of light.

This huge metal tower, called a ground station, sends radio waves to **satellites** and to other ground stations.

A fiber-optic cable can carry thousands of different telephone messages at the same time. A **network** of these cables can handle millions of calls every second.

By radio waves

If you are calling a person with a mobile phone, your message must be changed into **radio waves** before it is sent to the mobile phone. Huge radio towers, or masts, send the waves from one place to another.

Getting Messages

If someone calls when you are not at home, there are ways of making sure you do not miss your messages.

Voice mail

If you do not have an answering machine, the person calling can record a message on voice mail. The message is stored on a computer at the telephone **exchange.** When you get home, you dial a special number to hear your messages.

This machine links to your telephone. It can show who is calling, even if someone tries to call while you are using the phone.

Call waiting

If you are already using the phone and someone else tries to call, you may hear a special sound on the line. Call waiting is a **signal** that tells you that someone else wants to speak to you. Some phones also show the telephone number of the caller.

Telephone bills

Your telephone bill includes the cost of all the calls you have made and the cost of using the telephone line. You have to pay extra for services such as voice mail and call waiting.

You can usually pay a telephone bill by mail, in person, or sometimes even with a computer.

Faxes

"Fax" is short for facsimile, a word meaning "an exact copy." Fax machines send exact copies of papers by telephone.

Sending a fax

The fax machine **scans** a sheet of paper, line by line. It changes the pattern of light and dark into **signals.** The signals travel through the **telephone system** like a phone message does. The piece of paper itself does not get sent.

To send a fax, you load paper into the machine and dial the other person's fax number.

This man is getting a fax. His machine prints the copy line by line, as it is sent.

Receiving a fax

You need to have a fax machine to receive a fax. The machine receives the signals line by line. It changes them back into a black and white pattern, just like the original sheet.

Pictures and words

Fax machines copy a pattern of light and darkness. This means that you can send pictures just as easily as you can send words. But the machine sends only in black and white. It cannot send in color.

Mobile Phones

A mobile phone, sometimes called a cell phone, is one that you can carry with you and use when you are away from home. It does not have to be connected to an **exchange** by wires.

Radio signals

Mobile phones send and receive calls as **radio waves.** The waves are passed on by **antennae** on tall masts.

Mobile phone masts are often set on the tops of hills or high buildings. Each mast can serve a wide area.

A skyphone in an airplane links to the phone network by satellites.

Antennae

Each mast sends and receives radio waves from all the mobile phones in its area. If you move from one area to another, a computer switches the **signal** to the antenna in the new area.

Text messaging

Many mobile phones can send and receive written messages as well as phone calls. This is called text messaging. You can press the numbers on the phone to make letters, but the screen can show only a few words at a time.

Computers

Telephones are also used to connect computers to the **Internet**. People can send messages called **e-mail** and find out information on the **World Wide Web,** a huge collection of information stored on powerful computers.

Modems

Each computer must be linked to the **telephone system** by a special box called a **modem.** The modem allows **signals** to pass between the computer and the phone.

Some phones can connect you to the Internet to search for certain information.

E-mail

An e-mail is a written message from one computer to another. Some mobile phones now have a small computer, so they can send e-mail and even link into some parts of the Internet.

Videophones

With a videophone, you can see the person you are talking to. These phones use video cameras and the Internet to send pictures, the same way that television pictures are sent.

In the future, more mobile phones may use the Internet to show videos and moving pictures.

27

Telephone Times

Here are some important events in the history of the telephone.

1837 Samuel Morse invents the telegraph, a way of sending messages in code along wires.

1876 Alexander Graham Bell shows the first "talking" telephone to people in the United States.

1878 The first telephone **exhange** is opened in the U.S. It connects 21 people.

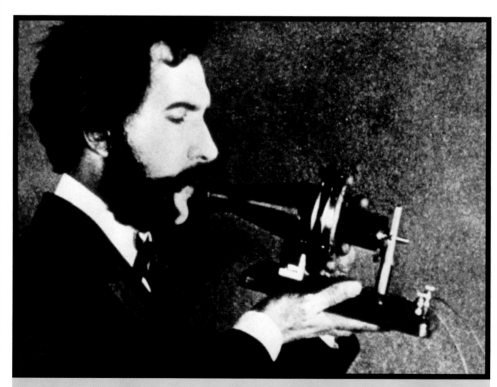

Alexander Graham Bell used his early phones to set up the first exchange in Connecticut.

1902 The first **fax** message is sent between Munich and Berlin in Germany.

1962 The first communications **satellite** is launched. It beams telephone calls and television pictures across the Atlantic Ocean.

1979 The Swedish company Ericsson introduces the first mobile phones.

1990s Millions of computers are connected to the **Internet** through the **telephone system.**

The large phone is one of the first Ericsson mobile phones. New ones are much smaller.

Glossary

accountant someone who keeps financial records for a company

antenna (more than one are **antennae)** metal rod or wire that can send or receive radio waves

e-mail written message sent from one computer to another

exchange place where telephone signals are sent from one telephone to another

fax exact copy of a document that has been sent by a fax machine through the telephone system

fiber-optic cable kind of cable that carries messages as light signals

Internet worldwide network of computers

modem box that changes computer signals into telephone signals, and telephone signals into computer signals

network system of telephones or computers that are linked together

operator person who works at a telephone exchange and helps to connect people's telephone calls

radio wave invisible wave that travels through air, space, and many other objects

satellite object in space that travels around Earth. Satellites can be used to send radio, telephone, computer, or television signals.

scan to read electronically

signals change in electricity or other energy, often used to send messages

telephone system many telephones linked to each other through telephone exchanges

transmitter instrument that sends out signals

vibrate to move back and forth very fast

World Wide Web huge collection of all the information stored in websites on the Internet

More Books to Read

Aliki. *Communication.* New York: Morrow/ Avon, 1999.

Alphin, Elaine Marie. *Telephones.* Minneapolis: The Lerner Publishing Group, 2001.

Fisher, Leonard Everett. *Alexander Graham Bell.* New York: Atheneum Books for Young Readers, 1999.

Index